# DEAD LETTER OFFICE

# DEAD LETTER OFFICE

Selected Poems

## MARKO POGAČAR

Translated from Croatian by
### ANDREA JURJEVIĆ

INTERNATIONAL EDITIONS
Barbara Goldberg, Series Editor

THE WORD WORKS
WASHINGTON, D.C.

THE WORD WORKS
P.O. Box 42164
Washington, D.C. 20015
editor@wordworksbooks.org

The publication of this book is supported by a grant from the
Ministry of Culture of the Republic of Croatia

Cover art: "Dead Letter Office"
Library of Congress Prints and Photographs Division
Cover design: Susan Pearce Design
Author photograph: Hilal Kalkavan
Translator Photograph: Forest McMullin

ISBN: 978-1-944585-41-9

# ACKNOWLEDGMENTS

With gratitude to the editors of the following publications in which these poems appear:

*Adelaide Literary Magazine*: "Romeo of Meat" "About Poor
     Weather," "Settlement (God and Cashier)," "Porch,
     the Emptiness of Windows" and "H. C. Andersen,
     Boulevard 50, Classic"
*Arkana*: "Man Dines in His Father's Slippers"
*Balkan Poetry Today*: "Man Dines in His Father's Slippers"
     and "Scabs"
*Birmingham Poetry Review*: "Library Fire"
*DIAGRAM*: "From the Cattle and Sports Management Manual"
*Juked*: "History"
*Natural Bridge*: "Barrel, the Night's Habit" and "July,
     Incomplete"
*Pleiades*: "An Object (Lost, in Its Complex Text)," "To Neighbors
     (This Morning My Flesh Is a Half-Staff Flag),
     "It's Lovely," and "Every Woman Adores a Fascist
     (For Dreamy Housewives)"
*Poetry Daily*: "Barrel, the Night's Habit"
*San Pedro River Review*: "Wild Palms" and "White Lie"
*The American Journal of Poetry*: "Archdiocese Chronicles"
     and "Saturday, Ruin"
*The Chattahoochee Review*: "Pursuit" and "Pretty Obstacles"

# CONTENTS

# III

# PREFACE

Croatian poet Marko Pogačar grew up in the 1990s when Yugoslavia was at the height of its internal dis-solution. For many years Yugoslavia was a stable country. But after Tito's death, bitter ethnic, religious and political rivalries erupted, eventually resulting in war, ethnic cleansing and the most horrific fighting on its territory since the end of WWII.

Croatia has gone through many changes throughout history. It was a duchy (875), a kingdom (925), had a personal union with Hungary (1102), and was threatened with invasion by the Ottomans (1527). To avoid being absorbed into the Ottoman Empire, the Croatian Parliament elected Ferdinand I of Austria to the Croatian throne, thus joining the Austro-Hungarian Empire. Eventually, through many more historical vicissitudes, it joined its neighbors in the Kingdom of Yugoslavia in 1918, continuing in an uneasy union for decades.

Skipping ahead to the 1990s, the six former Yugoslavian republics' declared drive towards independence grew to the point of their division, not without mayhem and agonizing pain: first, Slovenia declared its independence (1990); then Croatia (1991); then Bosnia-Herzegovina (1992); but in a never-ending spiral of disintegration, the Bosnian Serbs declared their own areas an independent republic. Years later, Montenegro also declared independence, breaking away from the rump remnants of the Yugoslavian state. Serbia became independent in 2006. And in 2008 the ethnically Albanian Muslim province of Kosovo declared independence from Serbia and gained recognition from the U.S. and most European states.

In light of Croatia's extraordinarily turbulent recent history related to Yugoslavia's inherent and eventually unrelenting strains, one wouldn't expect Pogačar's poetry to be filled with light—in fact, darkness is its overriding tone.

The first poem, "Man Dines in His Father's Slippers," lays out Pogačar's territory: "...stupidity, stupidity is at the heart of this world." The stupidity of fighting over ethnic identities, religion (Roman Catholic, Christian Orthodox, Muslim), borders, the course of the Danube—in fact, "What used to be the borders, is now you."

But who is "you"? the poet himself, his father, a lover, the reader? All or none of them? This is perhaps what translator Andrea Jurjević means when she states in her introduction that Pogačar's work is universal, not personal, or least not limited by the personal.

And his work can even be funny, in a mordant, absurdist way. Take the title of that first poem: "Man Dines in His Father's Slippers." "Dines," in English translation, suggests a rather formal meal. But the meal is eaten in slippers, his father's slippers. Has his father recently died? There's no evidence in the poem. Does it matter where readers travel in their associations?

Pogačar's poetry appeals because of what it is not—it is not conventionally beautiful, or lyric, or concerned with landscape. The pleasure is in the inventiveness of its nonsensical juxtapositions: "now that I'm alive I want quick and odd things / bones of leaves the green skull of an apple / heart beating in a less boring rhythm, yet still beating."

And still traveling. Take "Magellan, Home Alone." Magellan awakes after a drinking spree and "sails" in the direction of the fridge, "an explorer in search of a new world." It turns out that the world is a "watermelon/ seen from afar through a silk stocking." The poem continues the metaphor: "inside each seed, like in a town hall, a dead man keeps court/with his habit of silence..."

The poem ends with a question: "how does so much rain fit into the sky above such a small town?" One could ask how does so much hatred, bloodshed, rancor, revenge, rebirth fit into the sky above such a small country?

But Pogačar's work is not depressing either—the pace is too frenetic, even manic. We're too busy trying to keep our balance, racing to keep up with the language.

It's a chaotic, unpredictable ride, much like the history of Croatia itself, which is nothing if not turbulent. Best to hang on—it's worth the trip.

*Barbara Goldberg*
*Washington, D.C.*

# TRANSLATOR'S INTRODUCTION

Marko Pogačar is an astute, sharp-witted poet with a kind of punk-rock sensibility. He reminds us that god(s) don't exist, that we have to find our individual paths in life, and take responsibility for it. He tells us to declare a war on those in power who act like god, to uproot from the plague of patriotism, nationalism, and opportunism. He also tells us to learn how to accept mortality, our own and that of others, and to try to love, in all possible and impossible ways.

Poet, essayist, short story writer, and a respected literary critic, Pogačar was born in 1984 in Split, Yugoslavia. Somewhat of a literary nomad, he divides his time between Austria and Croatia, as well as frequent globe-trotting to various literary engagements. He lives by Rosa Luxemburg's words, "those who don't move don't notice their chains." Pogačar's poetry often explores various individual and collective restrictions in an astute, musical, and at times brilliantly wry manner. His appeal is always universal, never exclusive to the personal experience.

Pogačar grew up in a typical middle-class Yugoslav family. His mother was a post office clerk and his father an officer in the Yugoslav Army. Like much of his generation, he was formed, as an individual and a writer, primarily by the Yugoslav cultural space, Yugoslav music, literature, film, visual arts, and so on. He came of age in the 90s, the decade mutilated by the brutality of the Yugoslav wars.

Yugoslavia, formed after World War II when Tito and the Partisans (guerrilla forces led by the Communist Party) helped liberate the region from the German rule, was a federation of six republics: Croatia, Serbia, Bosnia and Herzegovina, Slovenia, Macedonia, and Montenegro. Following Tito's death in 1980 and economic decline, tensions emerged. Politicians also engaged in heavy manipulation of nationalist feelings, which had been present for centuries. The region was composed of a large number of ethnic groups, primarily divided by the different republics, each group having strong religious ties intertwined in their ethnic identity. This already present divide resulted in Slovenia and Croatia seceding in '91, as did the Muslim government of Bosnia and Herzegovina later that year. The next several years were marked by the most violent bloodshed since World War II. Much of this violence was aimed at the ethnic cleansing of the regions, leading to a death toll estimated anywhere between 100,000-200,000. Reports state there were about 2.4 million refugees and 2 million people who were internally displaced.

However, Pogačar's influences range far, from the New York School of poetry and the American underground to Paul Celan, Tomaž Šalamun, Roberto Bolaño, Thomas Bernhard and Peter Handke, as well as Marlon James, Ingeborg Bachmann, René Char, John Berryman. The list would be incomplete without musicians such as Lou Reed, Bob Dylan, and Joe Strummer. Pogačar doesn't differentiate. The best poem, he says, is omnivorous; it feeds on every source, without differentiating. Perhaps that's the reason why his poetry contains a strong affinity for the absurd, a sharp, hyper-lucid fluidity in its perceptions, and a robust punk sensibility, primarily seen in the musicality of his poems, disregard for grammatical conventions, and the interrogation of the dynamics between an individual and the collective.

While preoccupied with abstract concepts, and the practical application of those concepts to everyday situations, Pogačar doesn't fail to bring up questions such as: How to survive without dying? How to make art? How to write engaged political literature that never slips into the realm of manifestos, and instead keeps the poetic function dominant? He explores the idea of literature, the process of and approach to writing. And he believes that there are two inseparable topics we should never stop talking and writing about: capitalism and fascism.

However, regardless of how vocal Pogačar's viewpoints are, he is not terribly preoccupied by themes, but rather with the manner of their execution, the abundant possibilities when it comes to poetic expression. It is not important what the poet writes about. The what is secondary in poetry. Many poets' work tends to revolve around the same theme. What's changeable and of key importance is the poetic how, the poet's individual manner in which they write a poem — the art of it.

## About the translation

Pogačar's poems are political and philosophical, explosive, and disruptive. At their heart is a kind of anti-authoritarianism and non-conformity, discontent, an air of rebellion against the establishment, and a full-on embracing of free thought. And yet these poems preserve their primary poetic impulses and identity. They are unusually eloquent, frequently funny, rich in memorable imagery and unexpected imaginative turns.

For example, in the poem "What the Lighter Said," the speaker, "the sun's apprentice . . . led by revolutionary intentions" visits Sunday school and realizes that the only thing that arrives from the seat of the church is darkness, and references Buenaventura Durruti, a famous Spanish anarchist: "I, the sun's apprentice, once closely followed Durruti, knew / a church in flames is the only church that enlightens." The poem ends with the speaker outraged by children being indoctrinated by church:

> I, the sun's apprentice, stepped on an upturned plastic potty
> and late into the night, glowing ever more brightly, yelled
> arise, you prisoners of the playground, arise
> you made small in the sandpit.

The address "arise" is a nod to "The Internationale," the original left wing anthem, honored by socialists and communists, written in 1871 by Eugène Pottier, Parisian transport worker, French revolutionary, anarchist and poet. The hymn opens with, "Arise, ye prisoners of starvation!/ Arise, ye wretched of the earth!"

According to Pogačar, for literature to achieve its political potential it has to be aware of its imminent political nature, invariable immersion in ideology, and its need to constantly question its own ideology. It has to refuse to be unaware, or to be an opportunistic platform for a hegemonic discourse. That is its very basic level of engagement. Only then does literature have a chance to persuade politically. Everything else is poetic or political kitsch. In other words, only engaged literature is literature.

There's no idling in these poems. They're noisy, mercurial, authentic. Their movement resembles a beehive; it is unpredictable and usually turned inward. The sound offers both a sword and a shield. There is a thorough investigation of sound, language, and meaning. For example, in "Barrel, the Night's Habit," Pogačar says, "no bridge arcs the tongue and it's impossible to cross it." Tongue or language is a stranger, and we are, somewhat paradoxically, strangers in our own language, that same language which binds us. And yet this same language facilitates a distinct auditory pleasure in these poems, a cacophonic clamor, a cry, a complement to the resistance and protest.

Another point on the musicality is that Pogačar uses punctuation primarily as a musical tool. Grammatical rules do not matter one bit in his poetic work. Instead, punctuation is an important constructive parameter and a device for creating the rhythm of a poetic text. Without rhythm there lacks a poetic nature. In some of Pogačar's poems punctuation carries full semantic value; at those times punctuation (or the lack of it) is as important as the lexicon. At times the placement of a comma says more than words. Some poems simply have to remain open, not bound by periods, Pogačar claims, while other poems require final punctuation.

Pogačar often methodically uses internal rhyme and organizes the rhythm of each line with utmost care. He often achieves that by carefully harvesting the musical values of sounds such as č, ć, ž and š. These poems (originals, at least) resemble shrubs, wild tangled undergrowth of diacritic marks and dissident Slavic letters.

Many of these poems address a you. This you is not directed to an actual person; rather, address is the function of text. In that sense, Pogačar strongly believes in T. S. Eliot's Impersonal Theory of poetic coding, where the poet, as a medium, or a vessel, is not concerned with the personal, but rather escapes emotion and personality. This doesn't imply a certain coldness of a poem or detachment of a poet, quite the opposite — it creates a text everyone can find themselves in, at the very least as an absence.

Some of these are dense, demanding poems. However, we should not force interpretation with the intention of finding the meaning. Instead, as Pogačar says, the importance of a poem is derived from its truth, or multiple truths, that the reader is to realize organically. While this at first might sound slippery, the interior truth of a poem, its total tautology, is usually clear to the reader. A poem in that sense cannot lie. A poem whose truth we cannot fully know is a poor poem, or is not a poem at all.

Finally, many of these poems concern the concept of borders, at times physical, and often limits of language and poetry. They seek, with much vitality and vibrancy, to expand and traverse said borders. Borders, after all, are meant to be crossed. And poetry here acts as the aggressor, in a way, that keeps expanding, redefining, shifting the borders. Like

Wittgenstein says, "The limits of my language mean the limits of my world." That's at the heart of Pogačar's poems. And now they stretch the limits of the English language.

*Andrea Jurjević*
*Atlanta, Georgia*

I

# ČOVJEK VEČERA U PAPUČAMA SVOG OCA

Što su bile granice sada si ti.
bio je svibanj dubok i ravan
cesta raskopana zbog radova, snijeg
suh i odjednom.
da kažem otvoreno:
nikome nisam dugovao ništa.
stajao sam u dovratku, voda
smrzla od straha močila mi je leđa.
a kad sam sklopio oči vidio sam
kokice jure ka svojoj soli i znao
ponekad noću pocrne, kao brabonjci.
ušao sam da se suočim s mučnom slikom:
ne ljubav, glupost, glupost je srce svijeta—
i sad u tim papučama unutra jedem i plačem,
samo jedem i plačem u kući.

# MAN DINES IN HIS FATHER'S SLIPPERS

What used to be the borders, is now you.
it was May, deep and flat,
the street gutted with roadwork, the snow
sudden, dry.
to be frank:
I didn't owe anyone anything.
I stood by the doorposts, the water
frozen by fear soaked my back.
and when I closed my eyes I saw
popcorn rush toward its salt and I knew
some nights the kernels blacken, like droppings.
I entered to face the sickening scene:
not love, stupidity, stupidity is the heart of the world —
and now in those slippers I eat and cry,
only eat and cry in the house.

# BARREL, THE NIGHT'S HABIT

I was dead and indigo-blue
delicate as a tin can when I was born
a can of fat and bones, a bundle of breeze
shoved out of the black bed of a mother

tongue was a bay miles away
voice a bramble tightened
between the sun and the tricky task of passing

I was such a tin can, a divine scab
a scar on the skin of March, moist and late
that is the fire brigade of sleep

then I was a harvest, beginning of a cycle
that seems like an ending but isn't
like TV shows start with familiar scenes
and a worm enters a fruit to bloom

no bridge arcs the tongue and it's impossible to cross it
just swim and swallow and spit dark liquid down the teeth
liquid dedicated to silence

mother speaks correctly I mostly reject
now that I'm alive I want odd and quick things
bones of leaves the green skull of apple
heart beating in a less boring rhythm, yet still beating

I'm still that tin can and will again be dead and indigo-blue
when beside you a bent nail hammers me
love painted like a corn crib and a country stop
in summertime when hot trains tear and sow and tear again
that barrel, the night

# SYNTAX

Night after night, we swallowed the sun and our fists.
we, the cure against the virus of death,
would wake and visit the market
fry eggs with bacon,
tie hours into tiny knots
so that finally, when all's straightened out,
we'd have more time, enjoy it like a priest enjoys a boy,
like the woods drink the first sprinkle of rain.
we, mammals loyal to our reflex,
laid down one law — orthography —
forgetting there're no full stops in love, just series of commas.
with newsprint-blackened elbows we paid heed to
the existing revealing their names,
and the new shivering under the southern skin:
the living were cold, distant, eggs chirped, newspapers rustled,
the dead were near.

# SUNDAY COLLECTOR

My heart carried an endless Sunday
like a muffled murmur.
with each heartbeat time ripened into a song:
autumn curled up in every corner, stuffed hands into pockets,
chestnuts into newspaper cones. the deception of leaves kept winning.
chestnuts, still hot, rushed into hungry throats,
newspapers awaited a force stronger than wind, stronger than fire.
awaited the hand to pick them up, as if all the longing of the world
gathered into just three of all the things tied to old newspapers:
crumple them up and stuff them into empty shoes,
fold them into hats and send them to a random housepainter.
reuse one of the hats, perhaps the largest, turn it into a boat
for an imagined child to send down a stream into a land
where God is not boundless but mute. and there's nothing there.
nothing but Sundays.

# LIBRARY FIRE

I wrote cold poems separate from the world,
distant from you. literature was a full archive,
a thought detached from the heart. verses, bloodless
like oil-filled birds, briefly burned over daily routine,
glowed ghostly like a fridge at night, seduced
with the desire for mass to become energy, energy mass,
for all to settle into a quiet herbarium.

I watched you and the world get old apart from me,
having fun. I didn't write about that.
I didn't take notes. you could basically say I got up
and slept, got up and slept, for years I got up and slept
without jotting down the chronicle of your absence, sketching
life as a winter landscape, a snowstorm. all that
slowly slides into the past. all breaks away like a bandit dog.

under the skin, like a boil, blooms the library fire.
life draws into parched pages. maybe manuscripts don't burn
because the last shade of reality left them:
like living together, exchanging small affections, vegetable stews,
spending Sundays in the bath tub, stealing books, crime novels
for reading in southern nights. here comes the season of lies:
I'll wear clean socks, learn languages, I have a huge penis, all that

so a thought could align with heart, so verses would smolder at ease
evermore. here comes the season of lies: the fridge doors open spilling
light on our calm life—our working class neighborhood, freshly
          baked pizza,
magazines in lieu of books—so there'd be time for the final chronicle,
you and the world under the same duvet. all outcomes of history are
          the same. all verses
depend only on you. grasshoppers munch and crunch, kettles hiss,
          a new dawn climbs—
the guillotines go up in smoke.

# THE LAST HOLIDAYS

The days rotted in calendar squares, forgotten
in their red and white fields, and we slowly faded
forgotten in our red-and-white country. it could've been
in pig-slaughter season; columns of fog snagged in low branches,
thorns by the roadside lurked for the sweaters of passersby.
a boy pulled a cat on a rope, mumbled,
you won't stay, so I'll punish you, tie you to a radiator
and you said to yourself: go ahead, tie it. and asked why
write about the weather, what's with all this autumn, what's
so crucial about it, there's plenty of weather even without poetry. write
about yourself for once, you said, then barked at the boy: drop dead.
well: I like Agota Kristof better than Agatha Christie,
I prefer lyric to confessional verse of Anne Sexton,
I dislike walking on a person's left side, I'm not paranoid, I don't
        believe in secrets
if I were to tell you more I'd have to kill you.

# ABOUT POOR WEATHER

This is no spring.
only flowers twisting tediously out of small cups
and bees singing linoleum and the carpet of wind. the air,
deep and heavy, draws under the grass and lifts
bellies of mice: in less than a day they
bare the body like a curtain and spread
bones and guts. this is no spring.
only the river rising and pantries
waiting to be filled with sheer news. here and there gods
coo from graves, like pigeons. and their people
gouge the eyes of other people, but at night, that happens
at night. it buds in daytime and birds return to the city:
song-heavy cables and shit-fertile soil tighten the throat.
hedges crawl to the sky. waiters bring out tables
and flies fall into glasses. green learns its language fast—
the reliable vocabulary of the cypress, letters of beech and birch;
even the dirt under fingernails is ready to bloom. still this is
no spring. it's nothing. there's no spring without you, enough
enough with lies.

# FROM THE CATTLE AND SPORTS MANAGEMENT

When a cow in pasture blacks out
drunk on rotten pears
plunder spreads from its rumen
like a long-restrained tongue,
reaches across the landscape and translates
the wasteland into a blind chronicle.

when playing soccer
with a cut-off human head
put a sock in it
so the teeth don't bite the air
the spit doesn't dampen the grass
or the tongue babble about justice.

# WHAT A LIGHTER SAID

I, the sun's apprentice, came down from a wild heart
and walked in led by revolutionary intentions
armed with a clear idea and my deadly tongue
into a preschool of a quiet working-class neighborhood.

Sunday school has started.
lined up by the blackboard, staggered like stairs, upright
like a celestial team during the rings of a divine hymn,
the children broke teeth on code words.

I, the sun's apprentice, once closely followed Durruti, knew
a church in flames is the only church that enlightens.
inside me suddenly something sprung from my master,
the grit with which the sun loses itself in work,
and I decided to melt children's fillings.

I, the sun's apprentice, stepped on an upturned plastic potty
and late into the night, glowing ever more brightly, yelled
arise, you prisoners of the playground, arise
you made small in the sandpit.

# MAGELLAN, HOME ALONE

You woke up sweaty and naked
muscles cramped from a drinking spree that lasted too long
and sailed in the direction of the fridge, sweaty and naked,
an explorer in search of a new world.

it turned out the world is a watermelon
seen from afar through a silk stocking
under its core bloody magma, sugar cooled into envy
tosses seeds in its sweet love.

inside each seed, like in a town hall, a dead man keeps court
with his habit of silence, his test of stillness
until a knife floods rooms with the syrup of warm spring nights
and clerks, abandoned by everyone, run before the first drops
under the roof of a provincial post office.

from there, the haughty and dry watch pigs swallow the world
and the storm rinses out its map; they ask: how does so much rain fit
into the sky above such a small town?

# THE LONG ARRIVAL OF LIGHT

Again the deception of spring. the dawn climbs slowly,
pants up the stairs like my neighbor, fat since she was a child,
a person of your age, whom you've never seen as a woman.
the long arrival of light. the days denied their allowance,
skinny days on minimal pay ended with their own shift:
the assembly line of the wall calendar says *spring*,
incontestably, though it's just another fresh winter's wound.
here, up north. up north where, under the sun,
looming up, flames of the gas heater fuse with the blue
stove flames on which simmers coffee
and blood sausages in a blue, polka dot pot.
and that's how we overlook the betrayal of the calendar
following a decree of our inner party, fixated
on the base that nears its ending. *crashing an after-party is like
crashing a memorial, but more classy*, you murmur over a mug
as love supplies dwindle and coffee washes the night sediment
replacing it with a sediment of its own. I part the curtains then,
and see the dawn now truly holds the sky,
tight and restless, beautiful like a burning guillotine,
the coup of coal.

# TRAP

I followed him for hours. it was Tuesday, the clouds
withdrew, the wound burned under the skin, bright,
the worm of doubt having not nagged yet at his tight heart.
I breathed down his neck. watched him buy sandwiches,
looking over his shoulder; always the path was clear, me at his heels,
       inaudibly, just
to get closer to his wound, wanting to steal it.
a wound is a wonder. the body's bulge jutting out in soft death.
       wound-lottery,
a postcard from the flesh, I whispered while the sun lifted the wall
       of dawn
between a storm and the wound that throbbed.
I followed him for hours, and then lost him. without him love
wanes. without him there's nothing. a word budged and pecked and
took off and all I heard was a crow caw inside the wound, its impossibly
slow blooming. I looked for him until the first snowfalls.
I lay skin under knives, forehead on rails,
I licked the bone and the coal and an icy fence so the tongue
would give birth to its own wound, so I could quit. I knew the fast one
becomes the white prince of space. I knew the early bird catches
       the wound.

# WATCHING A WOMAN WATCH A WOMAN
## AT A DRIVEWAY

The car must be close by now. the round pocket mirror
refracts a ray of bright morning light
and what this woman sees in the glass looks like a dream —
a fetching young woman, a patch of green, a wheeled suitcase,
a slice of sky that starlings fly over.

inside me fumes the affliction of future
and I see a woman facing her fall, sad for not having courage to leave,
frost starting to stick to weeds. the taxi never arrives,
the suitcase serves as a handheld closet; the mirror ends as any mirror,
starlings as starlings when a cat pounces.

buttoned into my affliction, leaning onto the windowsill,
watching the woman watch a woman at the driveway
I pour sugar into tea and stir until it fully dissolves:
what's this penchant for weather, I ask, such a sudden talent for death;
has the season arrived, didn't we have different talents?

# OFTEN ASKED QUESTIONS

A simple evening. no unexpected
late meetings in the Tajga bakery
encounters that briefly make small town life
reminiscent of a scene from a cold-war crime novel:
like bribed spies, we gather around
plastic tables slouched over two cream pies
and the waiter, unbribable, like a retired cop,
jumps at a third call, crying out: right away!
dreamily levitating in the neon light,
like an icon or a saint needing protection, you said:
anoint it with honey. there're no program interruptions,
no final games, what's done is done.
manic needs come first:
wash the cups once again, check if
documents are in their place, windows tightly shut,
fold the clothes and lay them over the back of the chair.
ready for whatever is emerging, darkness, sweet meetings,
hours of lounging, begging the most asked questions:
how does one come from a pair, where's that snow, how much
longer is all this going to last?

# AN ORANGE APOLOGIZES TO THE
## TOWER OF BABEL

Where've you been? long time no see at this dangerous seashore —
I say to myself. but think of the tight north room,
the bed with a heavy body embroidering
a sheets with roses which growl at me from the seams,
bleached and sharp.

yet to speak is to sin: speech is nothing but an archive of errors.
flies spit on light bulbs, your absence escapes words. it flakes,
together with nature, presses hollow stems into the skin.

you'll agree: perhaps death is just a misplaced full stop
a slip in a pit's heart.
there're psychics on TV news and fascists in minister's armchairs,
        you're gone
in front of the post office a frozen Stafford waits for a cumshot
online models snort dried out words, and oranges,
at dusk they swallow darkness, fend off the night: they don't give
        a damn.

# SUNDAY, EARLY AFTERNOON

I shove the night into an evil email
and send it to the entire nation.
still a song needs more;
it's too easy to depart this way.
what's needed, for example,
is to say: it's Sunday, early afternoon
somewhere boys shout
because their team won,
summer broke into the knees, lifted hair
which is mostly seen on girls.
to say to leave, to thicken into oneself
a lump of milk skin nailed into the sky,
while words under the table are twisted
like feet, scents soggy and dense,
mice of the soul. more. still more
is needed. and I enter the song swiftly
like a cock enters baby Jesus:
it's sizzling Sunday, early afternoon
and people maddened by light wait
for the morning to open the mail.

# METAMORPHOSIS

Where are you? I sensed your shadow under my feet,
for days sensed the shadow. to the north,
over dance floors, desolate dim rooms, in the darkness of an orange
in every handshake, coffee mug, every spam folder that very shadow:
and you nowhere to be found.

lit by the lantern of the world I walk
home to pour that into a twisted tongue. but a tongue
is quick: it turns at crossroads, at night it overtakes;
the axe of memory sits at the nape of the neck, and the traffic is
		jammed,
the breaking begins, and the tongue ends up like a hedgehog.

and how easy it is now, at the memorial of the tongue,
the tongue rogue and silent, to whisper to your shadow:
what if it's you I love, and the night is desperate
the optical cables are cut, cell phone carriers on strike,
and I don't know what to do with this news.

# SETTLEMENT (GOD AND CASHIER)

The world is a bookkeeper with a comb
in his shirt pocket, a gold band, a link

that's missing, a link
cut into the flesh of the finger, into a hog's axis—

bookkeeper, that world, with all his lice,
with his nettle shampoo helpless, oh fully
needless.

love, a somber cashier.
and then a trip, winter vacation on the Tisa, skating

across a frozen lake, in crazy eights,
in the symbol for infinity, in a dream,

in a dream about hogs it ends with a final fall.
the cashier eats croissants, cheese and cherries, alone:

the cashier under the sky. between her teeth stick
crumbs. in ears rings the clink of ice skates.

and in the matchbox, foul and empty, coffer for the dead,
god: god is an ATM.

# PORCH, THE EMPTINESS OF WINDOWS

There is a history. I tore a leaf,
ribbed and green between winters, dug my teeth in it,
swallowed from bitterness. outside heather bloomed.
the elderberry kneaded nostrils. somebody stowed
furniture onto a truck, breathed too tightly, the asphalt
was kissing with his naked stomach.

there, thorough the rain of belts you could see
water spilling over the crupper.
how they drag, how they lift, like oxen.
I stood there—under the Stop sign,
on the square that flees from the night, folds
with the dark into itself like a lily, under a shop awning
where phantom taxi drivers crouch. the leaves were brown then green
then again brown and snows readily poured themselves into rivers.

there is a history. space under the fingernails. I tore a leaf
from a book, white like a festive shirt,
and until late afternoon I copied letters from it.
the dusk gathered into a sentence: freedom isn't 447 from Rio
or a dumb bird, freedom had to be fought for—
while I read I pressed tea leaves into a clot
through a forest of signs a truck approached me
unreal, greasy from the night; the waters rose once more
and the snow, dirty, poured through fingers.

there through shoulder bones I saw foxes growl
at an unfinished house, porch that isn't there, the emptiness of windows,
there I wait for you.

# H. C. ANDERSEN BOULEVARD 50, CLASSIC

All day long I kept thinking about the pear.

I woke up feeling the ripe fruit
swell and tighten down to its core and pips
like a vast heart of the world.

noontime, the sun truly in its place,
instead of yellow I imagined brown and green pouring
love onto the crown of my head, into the hole
God drilled.

at the same time I thought of the pear in your mouth
and I don't know what made me happier:
the trail of saliva that, radiant, poured down your tongue
or that it happened because of the pear.
also sadness struck me, longing for something of yours,
but the thought of the pear pushed it away
sparing my dignity.

afternoons, I'm sometimes prone to do new things,
so I tried to meditate the pear out of my thoughts.
still I didn't manage to clear the head:
the parliament was in session nearby
so only nonsense came to mind
dangerous nonsense I didn't know how to use.

in the evening I was tired from thinking
yet even so, eyes closed, I saw the pear, fresh,
swaying in the hole of the window.
terrified I got up, because hovering things frighten,
I closed the window and drew the curtains, laid down
but the pear didn't disappear.

later, in the deep night, with my hand on forehead
it appeared all pictures of the world fit into one:
a pear, large succulent pear taking vengeance and mountains,
lumpy yellow mountains: my teeth its skyline.

# JULY, INCOMPLETE

Here is a city
a platter the night nears too slowly
a sizzling platter, yet the night still sinks

this is a large city
still rarely anyone throws a party

July

that pressure, the block under the year's head
the tragedy of our time.

here is a city, here is a city can you hear
the newsstands, one by one, lift their lids
rain at once turns to steam, our people in the sky
people in the chimney stacks

still I love days wiping away into yesterday faster
faster like furious hedgehogs flee
into a nightmare of greasy hollow hedges

yes, the sun increases across the scalp
and it's becoming harder to face the facts
the people are in the sky shackled by stars
like Gould up in Canada, in a whole forest of stars

down here it's July and the skin scorches
everywhere else is Croatia, one dumb boomerang
fires, lounge chairs, the hewing of song

when the clothes dry too fast
and death fits into the three dots
at the end of an incomplete sentence.

# PRETTY OBSTACLES

A house is a box.
there're various houses and various boxes, they say.
depending on needs, climate
spirit and other faults. there're so many
it's sometimes difficult to recognize them.

still, a house is a box, I say.
like a hot oven is the sun,
ribs a cage for the dreamless owl of the heart,
forehead a glass and each bone a flute. no.
I don't care in which order they arrived.

that's already the archeology of the house
and the philosophy of the box, or vice versa.
what's important are boundaries, if you want walls
and that those beautiful obstacles are everywhere.
every house and every box has to be able to be closed.

the key to success is in covers, in case of a house, windows.
stronger than doors, slyer; always more secret-prone.
chimney is a hole at the nape. an opening for air
pierced by an awl if a rabbit is inside, better:

an exhaust pipe, the exit of the living from life.
no. smoke isn't a soul. there's nothing dumber and more boring
than soul. smoke is what makes the house-box possible:
the treachery of walls. an invitation for the sky's opening.

# FROM THE CARNIVORE'S COOKBOOK

Like a kettle the world
simmers on the camp stove of the sun

the earth is water brought to madness
seasoned with death

and every dead man
every dead man is a heart of a chicken

ticking

II

# THE LAKE

*Again that tragic*
*Mixing up of things and folks.*

—Novica Tadić

1.


I am the lake, I set out
in the morning from the slow cocoon of the sun—
sink into myself as if into a silent room or despair.
plants nest in my chest
like wading birds nest in shrubs,
the eternal choir of grass blades.

I am the lake, a dark spot
a parliament of a billion sweet tears.
I dream mostly at night and when I drift
calmly like an island or night sky—
I dream of crisis and democratic changes,
wake up purging out of convictions, thick
lilies pour out my throat, lilies sticky
like lacquer.

I'm a good citizen.
on weekends I drive for miles
through spears of upright flowers,
and leave no trace behind. nowhere does one
part of me beckon another. no one ever
talks about that. what land takes from me, I give it,
what's withdrawn cannot be lost. everything beautiful
stays beautiful. never mind the sea.

2.


The path around my eye is a shackle,
an umlaut of grass and stone that dirt
uses to enclose and restrain me. I can't step over
or exit myself without changing,
cannot spill out. therefore I sing into the leaves.
climb on the tips of my toes, offer my neck to heights
until it sharpens into a toxic syringe, and from it
shoots a tongue, a birdless flock.

all of me is my voice. I lift myself up. leaves
leave their marks. I enter those breathing ears the way I enter a woman,
or an animal. and there's nothing else to be written —
those who sing themselves are sentenced with ears,
space that attracts and alienates; like doors, or wars.
the history of the world is the history of ears. if you knock
a street comes out with all its clamor and the night floods you,
cloaks you in nothing.

I was, clearly, a lord. so many rivers on their feet,
so much habit, harmless and dangerous, like love.
everything I brought now crouches inside someone else.
drifts asleep inside them while I talk to them. nonetheless
I am the lake. with the first rain, I slide back into my mute self—
the autumn carries winds from silent waters and soon
every ear floats on my surface, and sinks, rots at the bottom. no other
lake is the lake.

3.


I am here. I agree to my place
because place is the only distinction I have. I agree to it all.
my other mirrors in me and I no longer know
where I begin or where I end. I tear at my seams.
a flock of headless birds takes flight from me and falls on your
        chest. grass,
cows and clouds reflect in my wet plane. the clouds gossip
about their history because it's vast; it piles up like rocks and violence
in my district. I don't understand cows, and grass doesn't speak.

everything deserts me. trying to hold on is like
going out in a summer night, the city peeling off its coat, offering its ribs
to birds, from within and without.
if I try to hold on, I shiver. inside me resides a rapid
and locked room in which you sleep. I am all of your space.
I don't moo like a cow, I don't chew the cud,
I don't pile up. if I smile a swarm of bees jumps
and grounds every sound, every resistance to silence.

I don't consent to posterity. no place should contain
more than one kind of presence. the evidence are people, language
and disease. now the grass speaks, the sky's clear, and cows are
        incomprehensible again.
it'd be stupid to wake up one morning as a cow. how
hard it is to talk, and not to speak to someone. to pour someone's
green place from you. the place that's my pork chop. I'm here.
if I ever move, pull me apart and shove all but my fingers deep into
my throat and choke me. place is my fate: no one
has ever walked on me.

4.


What can the lake say about the lake?
first of all, I'm like an iceberg. I crouch cold and
alone and wait for someone to come by, kiss my hand.
then I spill over the deck, cover it for so long
it seems cherries start bursting into a bloom,
I then swallow December, and respond. I don't talk much.
those whom I know I tell the lake is a division, a dark stone
on the bottom of every jar. I don't talk to strangers.

what can a cow say about the lake? I get up in the morning, moo
and chug of water. all damn day I think of Tolstoy.
I imagine him undressing me, spreading my eyes and placing
a long, poisonous bolt between them. when I fall, when I finally
splay out, he wraps himself in all of his space, and takes me. for days
he doesn't approach me. I no longer graze, the grass refuses my
          body. the world
and things elude me. he tortures me with words. the lake is a conflict,
          a fast
animal; a sea separated from the sea.

what can a psychoanalyst say about the lake?
a mistake. whiteness arrives from all directions,
like a just love. once the tongue inside me knew all its words,
as a sheep dog knows its herd. it started with a trauma.
for days the tongue carried cherries, even though they didn't bloom.
          spring
was arriving as scheduled. my waters started warming up, a day-by-day
leveling out with the surrounding space, until it disappeared. who
finds it holds the right to speak. everything is the lake except the
          lake itself.

5.


Boredom. a mysterious infinite
drip of water. I've been here for years. so many
damned years I could stack them up to the sky
if the sky weren't just an iron fist,
a ribbon of rain that ties us. sometimes I think
ascent and shame are the most relative categories. everything that
ever climbed out of me came back down. it takes two to feel
       shame and I'm
at any given moment one, never both.

on weekends dogs arrive and spread me around. carefully,
take me into their mouths and swallow me, like a body.
then they run, disturbingly, release me through skin, yelps, marks.
complete in that thick scent, I transfer myself.
I take the best from genes and viruses, to form myself.
every time I wake up blue-eyed, I say: hello, sky,
who's your father? the sky nods and darkens into the night,
as if lulled by my soft, long silence.

boredom. an endless tennis match. a song yanked out of me
with pliers so I wouldn't flock into something else, a mole
or a cow. I tear at the seams. my dead sea gathers,
lifts, and rocks me, like a storm does. like a mysterious infinite
drip of water. to get up and do something wild, swell into a dark
      contour
so the entire sun fits inside me, sun that gets swallowed.
to refuse every order. a well is boredom:
I am joy.

6.

I am the lake, but what's that?
a dark valley someone burly and lonely sails,
a set of obtuse angles. the emptiness between
sparse drops of rain; when spring unfurls down nearby
hills, I'm the familiar and unfamiliar,
as just about everything else is. my foundations are unclear.
sometimes snakes, which even I recoil from, come out of me.
does that mean that deep inside me I'm a snake?

the lake is an egg. everything that comes out of a shell travels
toward its bottom. sometimes butterflies hatch. a silver pellet darkens
the sky as if it's trying to rouse it. but even the blind know
it won't. sometimes pure greasy evil busts out of the shell;
one word replaces another, as if nothing has happened.
I shake myself down and straighten up, chase the word to the roots
of my teeth, until it introduces itself with its full name and admits
there's nothing to a name.

at the end of it all, what am I left with?
waking up every morning with my surface, watching
that snakes remain snakes, and I the lake. getting excited with the idea
that changes come from everywhere. perhaps have fun.
I'd fall in love if that weren't an English phrase
and I weren't so endlessly alone. I'd peel myself and layer by layer
give me to another; go numb. luckily, I'm so desperately hollow
and have no other language but the most beautiful one.

7.


I swallowed a village church, and climaxed
as if on Christmas. as if ants snuck under my skin.
first I mowed the foundations, then moved up,
licked bricks, frescos and their lasting goodness and when I
reached the steeple something spilled across my veins, something
thick and joyful, like fruit. one who picks fruit knows
a tree could've kept it. it lets go of it one by one,
like earth shakes us off little by little
without generosity.

so I swallowed that church. the congregation ran
toward the exit, which didn't exist. I went up too fast.
and I felt no guilt: I thought, somewhere over the sea
a butterfly beat its wings, a flock of dumb butterflies.
I thought there was a silver lining. the ceiling dropped
and the rest kept growing—all the candles remained
lit in water, and that plankton glowed across the horizon,
too wide to darken.

I then pulled back into myself. I bit my ankles
to stop myself. I swallowed one village church and now
a herd of bloated cows roams around my landscape. if I were to blow
into them, bagpipes would blossom. the bags would deflate and
the melody would haunt me, as if I were guilty of something. it's all
anatomy. how does a neuter climax? easy and fast. like
loosing one's mind, being born again, or overdoing it. as if we need
each other.

8.


Don't be thick and acrid. every so often I lick
you with my waves to soften you. dearest dirt,
lesson in discipline; can anyone swim in you?
spring is arriving, one of your pretties proofs:
waiters bring out round tables, the sun brings out
the round sun, shop windows change. no one knows
this many shapes of growth: even the smallest grain lifts you
toward the great lock of the sky.

don't resist. perhaps you're just a tired sea.
tranquil and inert on the surface, like a lizard: when you want
          something
you turn into a quick tongue and disappear. when I want
something so madly I turn every one of my rocks till I'm sick to death,
I dry out all my branches, just to find it.
if I'm left empty-handed nothing can console me.
then I take away from you. out of spite I spill myself,
intensely and softly, so I can reach you.

earthquakes denounce you. we're more alike on the inside
than you'd like to admit: for example, bugs walk over me,
and moles swim in you. plows and flowerbeds are proof
it's possible to sail you. to be honest, I've never
seen a fish inside you, but I've never trawled you. your fish
are great-grandmas of mine and I love them. when spring arrives
          lit in new
revelations, I bathe, swim with the living. inside you calmly
float the dead.

9.

A thick screen descends into my hair, everything dulls
and darkens. animals come out to graze. in their teeth
they carry a thousand pillars that propped the sky.
from now on the sky hangs off the stars. the grass
feels too heavy. in my folds
small round seeds ripen, bud under my teeth
again into the new form of labor. they sweat, dripping down warm
red thighs, like rainfall.

the cattle is gone. the darkness thickened so densely
I can't even mirror myself. the eyes of frogs are dark splotches,
a love negative. it's so quiet I dream. my mother
brings me apples: a large basket of apples. I lick them all
over to wash off their color. if I try to slice them,
make them bleed, break down into the landscape and tire.
apples, absolutely unaware, lie back in their weak history
like in a still life.

I wake up. blink as if I'm becoming an alien,
as if that'll trigger a gaze. the thorns caught a calf
muzzle and drink from it. raspberries smell unbearably.
in the air, like in a white clinic, floats the next day —
something else, a different, always reliable fatigue thickens,
gathers beneath wings. enough exhaustion and the wings spread,
        the bird takes off
and it's already morning. it's clear: nothing but apples
was inside the apples.

10.


Take me away. I'm only safe here.
an agent between two happy worlds,
calm until they touch. I so wish you'd
take me, I invented a name and a soul; a few
names, because I don't know which language you speak. a soul
sets its own boundaries: it's impossible to
calculate the surface of a soul. I am the hollow
rib, a pure eclipse, and I seem to be worried.

where will I find you? like God, when he's around,
borders every object, I border with you.
if I leave this dull line I'll no longer witness you:
we exist only when I'm a lake and you an endless Sunday.
only seeds prove you. opened up into one autumn
they float on my surface, the cradle of shadow, every future
growth that's your blossoming. that's why when
foul winds blow, flowers float in your wake.

should I contradict you, I have to forget every word.
stop and enclose myself. so: take me away. stick a big
straw into my thigh, let them drink me. pour this round
body into the empty bones and beaks of sparrows, let it
briefly rise, and then let it forever fall. there's nothing
for you in the pastoral. grass keeps growing, and on my floor, surely
a patch of dry land, animals graze. to resist you is to surrender:
like on the brink of a painful story about sleep.

11.


I read a book of French poetry
which is strange as I'm the lake, and don't speak French.
never again have I seen anything as
pointless and sad. Flowers of Earth. the sediment
that letters deposit like hard water in one's mouth:
I've heard so much about it and all of it was true.
the earth beneath me. the flowers above my eyes.
I held on so tightly to the book that I fell.

the moon melted pestles. I remembered that,
and cows drinking me, although it happens every night.
nothing could escape the moon's frame: someplace
someone knitted the scenery into a swelling
of dull and slow time. if somehow I were a road
I'd roll into myself like a rug, just to stop moving.
air already did that to the sound. and the sea of radio waves, the sea
of music and yelping kept beating against nothing.

I swallowed everything, unrestrained. I needed sentences.
any kind of sentence. and when they arrived, vague and dense
like a sloppy parade, the morning became a failed party,
a closed ice rink in a city winter. now the sun melted
the pestles, and I kept reading. I knew those were only
words, but I couldn't help myself—every word was true.
beneath me earth. above me flowers. music and its stems
on their way to another room.

12.


I am massive and irregular
like the head of Francis Bacon.
whatever happens on one of my shores
reminds of an administrative error: no one
can enter the trace of anything. that's
just one of the tricks of returning. also:
there's no ice-skating, or fine dining; nothing that demands
an unusual amount of balance.

the principle, whose name I forgot, stated
that volume is final. wrong again.
I contain more than myself:
the eternity of a law equals only the width of an error.
tricky. that'd mean there's no escaping irregularities.
indeed, everything around me straightens up—the browse lifts
its head, and the cows devour it, as if it's their last;
everything living buds beneath and rises.

oh, big chiropractic sky!
pinned by the sun rays to the expanse, I waited
for the night wanting everything to stay clean and tasteful; I wanted
          nothing
unsavory. I wanted to leave in style. to leave myself
the way girls have always left me: quickly
& easily. there's no return. no consolation in your tongue.
the causes of this unforgivable vastness are worthy of a lawsuit
and deadly for all present. so. everyone gets what they deserve.

13.


Fear is a minor angel,
a little Goebbels who died in sleep. my
shores were once a long and gentle avenue, a curved
dagger in God's thigh. that clump
of beard and orders is lake's eternal enemy.
once he trudged into the lake like into the woods at night
and from there let a sickening, snowy growl. no doubt
the certain someone hates the lake.

with the arrival of water all the fast and wise
animals disappeared, and the slow and stupid ones stayed
the same. I lifted myself to the spot in which
the return was just that: an autumn path for the blind.
scared and naked I stood
with myself as if in a narrow mirror, watched
how suddenly something lowered onto me,
an abandoned voice; a missing body.

all that the lake saw was a litter
of dangerous dogs. let's just say: it suffered
a necessary depression, an excess of depth and all that water.
now suppose everything's a lie. over there's
a dry and pleasant picnic, lots of drinks and music and God
but the lake jumps off the bridge. inside it a mute and free fall,
under it a dull and endless bottom, like the Croatian senate. the
        landscape
lowers the heads of animals toward dirt. roots continue to rot.

14.


All around the lake,
from every direction, suddenly a stink of fraud.
patriotism arrived from somewhere and now cows rise flags.
the grass prepares its dress: fast and white
trains take away their young and soft to a moon,
the blunt hole in your tooth. however you look at it:
this is the first mass
migration of plants.

the lake is confused.
once the entire sky, like a forged lid,
was its special eye. what it
saw is too awful for words.
then the present arrived: the forming
of the independent democratic republic of cows. the lake lies
in itself as if in a truth and keeps its long, tight silence.
it forgets the foundation of every truth is the body.

that space is the only box of love. however, a lake
has a record because of revolutionary activities:
it believes in self-governance and *cannot stand* Christians.
so, what will happen to the lake?
warm and empty muzzles sink into it,
swiftly darken it. the sky is veiled, like a large, festive table;
the secret police breaks in and drinks into oblivion. in the morning
bloated cow guts cover the surface. so: death is homeland.

15.


I am the dirty, godless lake,
filthy pig of a lake. on Fridays I keep
fish inside my mouth, so Christians can't eat them.
I fast when I want. I use protection. on Sundays
I plow all my shores out of pure spite, place
my hand on your hair and fall asleep. nothing else moves.
cows devour their own legs. grass cuts the wind and freezes it
so peace could truly be dark, and movement louder.

I dreamt I evaporated. my topic silenced other
topics and then disappeared. too wide at first, it ran through the
            woods,
the valley of murmur, as if someone recognized it. I yelled:
wait, I'll hide you inside my word, and someone
willing and happy will handle it further. to which lake does God
            travel to?
I don't know, I said and turned away. everywhere the month of May
carried ripening. and dark dots that exited seeds closed
every night, decidedly, as this one.

I'm here. hairless I rest in front of your grass
like in an archive. song momentarily fills the plain:
sickles set out to outnumber us. thick birds
descends down their blades, and shepherds stay indoors. for days
I'm an expectant strawberry you carry on your tongue and now
            shamelessly
and godlessly I wander the countryside as if rolling around a big
            sieve. this too
will end. when my eyes are no longer eyes, love me
and have no other lakes.

III

# WILD PALMS

Loving, that's easiest, everything else is tough.
much time has passed: days have begun to cramp.
shopkeepers are cloaked in coats, priests in lies,
the night crowd is mangling the only live lightbulb, down
in the south end. what else do I notice?
the songs are becoming shorter.
and your eyes enter them as if entering stadiums
carrying flares. wild palms lurk
inside pockets. waiting for their turn, they squat
like Slavs in tracksuits in front of supermarkets
while the north plots a revenge, and silver counters
shut with a bang. the still life of a space. the pressure of blood.
as for the rest? breakfast goes to a cat, aorist to a verb,
gods to the poor. a cold country.

# WHITE LIE

Learn languages I don't know, talk to me
about things I don't want to hear.
be the link to the world of boring facts, such as
Sunday is a Sunday, Croatia Croatia
pension that keeps us alive.

at the same time be the strong eastern border,
a hood blacklisted to pizza boys.
be the stamp on the skin of a passport, a release letter, also
the one who doesn't play tombola, who plants hedges
so life would remain life, and a secret a secret.

learn languages I don't know, talk to me.
escape with your cat to the library, drink too much coffee,
adopt common words. tell me nothing in French,
tell me death in Polish: talk and nothing will remain as it was
once again everything will be different.

# MARKO'S SQUARE

Something's happening, I don't know what.
a rib cage expands and tightens,
blood vessels narrow, those grooves, glands
secrete great bile over Zagreb.
such is the sky these days: a nightmare
without a speck of holiness. a sketchbook with drawings
and pages yet to be filled, a hum
of a million moving feet.
'tis a nightmare, voices repeat, a nightmare
you repeat. the sharp slits
down which the rain seeps into steps; nails, surely fingernails.
wrists bound with leaves, because it's autumn
and such things pass painlessly. water boils
in pots. dogs blossom black. approach me and
you'll approach an obtuse evil: 'tis a nightmare, I repeat,
a nightmare, they repeat. the whole sky
pressed into a collar bone, and from sheer clamor no one
can hear another. all is new, all is foul,
and all in Zagreb. eyes, plates, things
over which we look at each other. all that's sacred and all that's sharp
all dogs, all of our viscous voices. the speech
of the city eager to bite, pine trees, a flock, something
in the air, under the earth, inside walls; something
above us and elsewhere. something's happening,
I don't know what.

# THROUGH THE KITCHEN WINDOW

A poem is a dense thing. a patterned curtain pulled
open with a single stroke,
black February the hand that calls me to the light, black spring the
      window;
underneath it blossomed a man

and we let the roots rise up: we churned
the sky like moles. it hadn't snowed yet,
ping-pong balls flew across the borders of space,
where the air thins and words, along with breathing, gain weight.
nothing extraordinary happened. kids in the yard blew
into whistles. women shelled peas, one of them
more a woman than most, surrounded by wind, under her feet
mice. on the other side, the sea was resting, but I keep quiet about that

a dense thing, dense—like a bone, like teeth-grinding winters.
icy air passed through me, warmed up in my throat and veins
and fogged up the pane as breath does. the window gathered the drops
I offered. it took all my writing. I know what my fingertips
cut into the scene like spit into snow, yet I don't mention it

in front the unknown in bloom, behind my back a woman
the wind sticking petals to face

# SCABS

The afternoon decays on its wobbly legs,
thaws, a calf that won't make it to the butcher,
a pasture bathed in bellows, it all
gathers in an evening awareness, dim
and self-admitted: cots on low branches,
blood on grass blades, only traces
of horns, like everyday poison; teeth strewn
over the dangerous district of the mouth.

I'm trying out the logic of small moves,
I observe: light is the measure for all things.
properly carved pumpkins,
cans open to an infinite encounter,
coated with rust that braces door handles, offers
a view on the mechanism of earth, its scabs,
arranged across the window sill.

it's hard to tell what begins. the light that crawls
along interior walls lays silent April shadows
pumpkins bloom, rust peels off: can winter with its
teeth crush stamens, and the pasture thaws under hoofs;
a calf rises, shakes off the drool, its muzzle
takes in the damp air; decaying, it seems, is finished.

now truly, from some dusty files,
the night descends on the sky: it slips it on like favorite shoes.
first left then the right one, then laces, and the night is
at last stable. finally the night is at its home, in the sky,
in the throat of a calf: the darkness rustles in my ears,
in treetops that lean over us too closely —
the weight of the night presses; the stamp that inks the papers.

# Romeo of meat

I stood bare-chested at the window, yelled
*I love meatballs, I love meatballs the best*, below headlights
cut the night like flak slices fingers in swordfish hunt
split the dark into halves. a dog, leprous and fast,
fell asleep in a puddle of its own shadow, a pool that moves
like the sleeping dog; how in slumber he's hounded
by thoughts of hot doe womb.

that warm stream a light, an intangible rug, pours between particles
like wedges. it squeezes through, rubs its back against white walls,
flashes off teeth, to end in the simple logic of the cypress.
an engine that revs in place
lifts sprigs of soundless smoke into the sky.
when the twisting light stumbles upon it,
in the clouds canned insects and moths, blazing specks,
float stunned. if the specks are traced with a greasy pencil
air flickers, a precise portrait of a blizzard, form and fleet of woods.

so: already the heroes who'll cut down the woods are lined up. whetted
axe blades shine like eyes, when licked by headlights. the silence growls,
the indraft of household aromas flee. just crickets' pairs of bellows and I
at the window howl *I love meatballs, I'm crazy about meatballs*,
and then someone, perhaps drunk, passes by, asks: *what kind do you love?*
and I say *with sauce, tomato sauce, ones in tricorn cans*,
*the only way to eat meatballs!* and the night burns black as an attic
      corner, cold
like a northern heart.

# LIGHT, SOMETHING EMERGING

Like half a peach
in its southern sweetness.
like raspberries, like peas.
a cow that moos
from the white federation of bones.
baked beans, earth kidneys,
meat for house pets.
what milk comes from
when roads are distant
and the winter's just and bitter.
like fish, ragú sauce, something.
we live quietly in the dark of a tin can
then someone lifts the lid
and lets in the sound and the light;
there, suspicious white light.

# HISTORY

A forest fire, that's when the forest burns.
heat from the southern sky lilts onto the treetops:
trees take in the delivery of leaf-wrapped light
like chicken swallowing dumb oats.
the trees are done then
except we don't know it yet. like a sow swallowing a fist.
a flame already rustles in the shirt pocket, within its
folds, and the day is decidedly brighter.
on the horizon, on its spine and its hairs
there are two suns; the wider one sniffs through the darkness.
it holds nothing for itself, goes nowhere.
truceless; it softens only when the smoke crawls
into the blind oats and remains there. everything will smarten up;
everything around me will soon become the sun,
the sun thinks while marrying branches with surrounding air.
squirrels and snakes race down the tree trunk toward dirt.
heat, not knowing its own name, sinks into soft
reality and the trunk pulses, mobs with birds
into the common madness. when from the trunk a beast bursts out.
it devours the bark and crests finally tear the surface.
in its deep silence, the trunk now crows.
it guides to another day too keen on passing.
the heat hastens down. it curls up, soundless,
someplace in the roots, a revelry cornered back to its beginning,
its wise youth. the fire craves itself.
it spreads across tall shrubs like dawn across the dark
sky, a greeting across a full and an empty room.
it licks the leaves, licks the bark, licks the roots, licks a little bit
of everything. and it becomes closer to one and all.
closer to the low and high, it starts out small
then loses itself in work. the world rumbles now:
amid air and earth remains nothing.
some animals have left, others have stayed.
above them the entire woods shifts,

intangibly, like the cleansing and crackling of hot springs,
a quiet impurity that flees yet adheres, condenses.
and all is somewhere and all is nowhere, and all is illuminated.
a forest fire, that's when the forest burns. a fire
is when it burns.

# ARCHDIOCESE CHRONICLES

The season retreats. the winds strengthen, the dampness makes
waves on the plastic kitchen floor.

it's time for the last register, of wandering in the suburban
woods with dogs, long weekends, books

forgotten in transparent summer bags,
passages never fully digested. I don't have dogs,

and some books I just don't get. I grumble and
discuss them with smarter friends.

near the season's end while the snow still squats in its sack
there is one bar in Zagreb, and we stick to it.

then that glacier sets off, damp and hot from our elbows,
and flattens the gas station with the sky.

the time of broken teeths, body soft as a turd.
I know I can't say teeths, still I don't know what to do with myself.

the horizon shrinks, afternoons become unbearable.
leaves, a carpaccio of memories, pass into a universal earth archive.

naked branches comb the stars, trams sorely squirm,
in silence. black nights for hearts, in the mornings southern eclipse.

I feel cashier windows tremble, tow trucks left in the grass;
holidays of former countries hum. somewhere there's still blood.

# LETTER

There were blood and a letter. after me a pack
of fast and furious, someone yelled get'im
I ran and swallowed slice after slice of the day
slice after slice of rain.

the black sock of the night fell
over the eyes of the newsstand thief; the city, an enormous coat
carried me in its pockets.

I ran, the night grew, familiar thawing
creased in lairs in holes, fear
sneaked into armpits. dogs took the outline of the father.
sycamores flaming the form of the mother.

such was an example: the north, January inside a fist
the city burned like a parliament session, joy
someone yelled get'im, I couldn't hear
I ran didn't turn back.

then darkness. blacktop under the fingers, the sky fused
like a scarf. get'im get'im cut the air;
I didn't turn back but I heard—the night a black gunshot
says love is a letter. I have it. blood colors strawberries.

# HOLIDAY

A pair of tiny dark eyes, the black pits of black
coastal pepper; an ear that's a wilted bay leaf cut
from a fascist's head, a muzzle, which I'd love to have.
the blind mouse gets it: a rabbit is cooking in the pot.
the flame underneath makes the body go mad, soft,
slowly shapeless. above it a heavy cast lid.
the heat makes sure the lid, that last hat to be worn,
bounces, like a ball, on the naked skull of the rabbit.
water tightened around the ankles frames the skin and
like love, swells the flesh. it crumples into an idea and departs.
all manner of things happen in that empty space. plumbs
have surrendered what they had. teeth bitten the enclosing winter,
that emptiness, the throat's tightened with stars. no one
can stop this; fire pulls the best out of everything.
from all over, like the exiled, arrives excess and the rabbit
knows: the hand turning up the heat erases a great hunger.
on the bottom of the pot sits satiety, a small revenge to the world;
a scout in night positions. death, a cure for the weight of bones.

# STILL LIFE WITH AN OBSERVER

Like a rug the tract of grassland rolls up
and presses into every bone.

the owner of the bones (a northern hunter,
cunning and covert in front of this picture)
sees in the frame a candle, four walnuts, a quince,
and something he can't identify.

one thing is certain: the unmistakable static of the view.
the wind remained behind absent windows,
locked up in a memory of the viewer.
the flame, fixed, doesn't flicker; walnuts don't stir.

and when the apprentice curator (boring on the outside,
on the inside interesting to female students of German)
opens the curtain and lets wild hot light into the painting,

the sun transfers the light onto the candle, the draft lifted
from the window carries a gust that catches the flame;
walnuts start a rolling riot. yet, the whole saga at once,
with the speed of a bite, becomes a statute of limitations

(the quince withdraws its scent, the hidden remains hidden)

# SATURDAY, RUIN

The day breaks and the sky falls
like a rotten pear
under the table.

worms crawl out
like waiters.

and unpaid tabs
lie one inside the other.

Maria enters, I say, hey Maria,
and she flashes her teeth.

from now on she squats and stops, squats
and stops, she decided
to carry her scent differently.

I lean toward pigs:
press meat into white meat
I close my eyes and see—

a hairy night sits on it all.

# TECHNIQUE OF A POEM

Croatia's first president is slain by amnesia
his posse by scalding soup and dead servants
who now avoid them; walking the city in the opposite
direction than death, I buy newspapers, I buy coffee at
the kiosk listen to my own salty charm, soft character
and some music; an average Croat is slain by cohabitation,
coping, gorging on snow — a wide, light blanket of smog
covers and lifts him up, along with all that autumn, its
darkened daybreak, the water that moves up your neck,
soft, lead-laced water; church is slain by constant quoting
of Christ, unconditional and everlasting love; a pig enters
the puddle of its own breath, a palmful of blood escaping
experience; a poem is slain by Drago Štambuk, a mother
the way detailed scriptures describe; nothing remains nothing
that sparkling scorched sun.

# AN OBJECT (LOST IN ITS COMPLEX TEXT)

He sits at his desk,
clutching a mug (the countenance)
of tea, brings it to his lips, drinks
and writes untranslatable verse.

without him, the sun would be frying
the entire stretch of the window—
this way its flash, god's gunpoint,
slowly strides along his front,
lowered forehead. without him words
remain rootless:

they travel between the body and time
into a strong nowhere. the process is long.
the meaning tiresome. he sits at his
desk, lifts the mug, drinks;

and that text unrolls like a long
tongue of a dog, haunted by a thought
about crops. from letters,
the dark fold of the city, rise voices,
they lift, descend and slowly whisper: good seeds

seek the rich soil inside him.

# TO NEIGHBORS (THIS MORNING MY FLESH IS A HALF-MAST FLAG)

Honey melts in tea, completely, unlike me in you
and you in classical music,

overly long phone calls, never a table when you need one
perpetually broken elevators,

steps unfolded into eternity, like a conversation about politics,
and when someone notices that totalitarianism and democracy

differ only in numbers
the picture disappears and all starts anew: voices drip from walls,

bodiless, and the night descends onto the palms, like a miner
into a drill-hole, still, the shoes left

by the door prove the living exist. but what does it mean to live,
while the winter arrives rolling like a cold breath out of my throat,

and builds a nest in a dark alphabet; all those strangers with familiar
names, rushing, an afternoon broken in two, like Korea,

the tea in which honey has already melted, inseparably,
and that viscous liquid is love; how do I get to you; how do I
        reach you?

# PURSUIT

A black dog chases a black bird. everywhere seethes
Tuesday. you and I run, oh tragic technique,
we stumble against roots, branches, our relatives
—we look up high,
dark fragrant matter, at that reality—
we carry newspapers under armpits, nothing
is our last post, we can't go beyond nothing.

and time, I say, time, you say
and everything spews—someone opens the door the dog flees,
and the world becomes a silver cage, and from it flees a bird.

the city then compresses, the whole city into one dirty window,
like a star into a black hole, like a dirty tissue into a pocket.

and all who walk with nothingness in their teeth, all with
their fear under tongues and a hand in cold hands,
all saints, bakers, secretaries and revolutionaries, pregnant ones, all
of them fast-frozen, watch—

fast as a rock a black dog chases a black bird, that's even faster.

# EPICS, UP THERE

Tremendous sediment settles, an immense puddle of tar.

the sky an empty coffee cup.
lipstick traces on teeth, the dangerous task of passing
goodbyes strewn across the room like tables on summer patios,
ashes in the shells of ears, mouths, fists,
vast ashtrays of the world.

it's all saints day, and I don't believe in any of them.
the fall of all things: the shedding of the body and time, a red calendar,
day trips, holes in void, nights, that are a chronic clotting of light.

from somewhere a sanding smell, the madness of fall's cold front:
            it rains
and it rains coffee, and we drink while we still can; while we're
            still here.

# It's lovely

It's lovely breathing the spring air at the Isonzo
and not be hungover.
absorbing the water drops and flowing inside them.
it's lovely to feel good. to have strength
for any form of faith that doesn't hurt another,
so, to not have.
it's also lovely to live at the Bosutska Street
and to believe it exists.
to go to the bakery every morning, to eat bread
over newspapers found in your mailbox.
it's lovely when mail finds you and when you can find mail.
finding, in general, is lovely.
to find a familiar face when you pass by the stadium
or a second-rate university. ridicule is lovely.
it's lovely to find a full stop.
a spreading knife which you lost long ago and now is silky.
a battalion of flaunting angels is lowering their iron ears
and that borders with horror. everything borders with horror,
and that's lovely, too.
to remove gum from the sole of a light shoe, the evil that
disturbs your balance and explains gravity.
Newton is lovely. Brodsky is lovely.
baricades are the heart of art and that's unbribable.
when perfect punk plays when Anna Karina's seen when
the moon is eclipsed when the flag is raised when
the Dead Sea parts. walking is lovely. drowning.
what's lovely for me is dangerous for another.
difficulty breathing in air filled with pine trees. speaking Croatian.
skating. the opposite is, as well, true.
windows that you can open and touch the clouds through
are lovely. Mosor is lovely too.
it's lovely to walk, to climb, to have faith in the peak, to know
what year the war ended when is the liberation day respecting
the Women's Day Mother's Day loving violets,

undressing. falling. being sure you're falling, and getting startled. waking up. cutting. firing unnecessarily long rounds of your name, being systematically tragic.

# EVERY WOMAN ADORES A FASCIST
## (TO DREAMY HOUSEWIVES)

Lightbulbs, instead of the sun these heavenly spheres of light. one day
you go blind from looking up.

you no longer see the walls. the dust decides to lower
its dead colony on your face. but even what looks alive

generally isn't, something died between eyes,
that's no longer you talking. the spaghetti are on the stove. the riot

of limp pipes, countless, dangerous asparagus. you accept the game:
you lay on the linoleum like in the dark scalp of a river,

waiting for his return. when he arrives the walls quiver.
he loves you like a sense of satiety, like a discipline. strictly and sternly.

loves you like he loves radio. the foam from the pot creeps onto
        your silent lips.
the night steps out of the afternoon skin, flies into the room like a
        butterfly, draws

under the rug together with figers. lightbulbs readily leave the sky.
something is born inside you, but will never live, you're full of time

and time rejects being filled with you: there're no eyes for crying, hair
leaves the scalp, love happens in the hallway, such are consequences.

# THE YEAR OF TEA

I've taken away and given as if I were
someone else. magnet is my default metal.
we always attract, but magnet makes more sense
in choosing, some things it simply rejects. I'm not
so stable. the sea crept into the clouds
and now it's sprinkling on me. a branch bends,
as if under the song of birds. yet no one's singing.
if the sun appeared on the street we'd have
a full rainbow, and the road would steam. something
is always born from steam. what a magnet receives
it keeps forever. a magnet is an implement for
defining love, even if sometimes it's broken. love
follows it. best case scenario, if the sun rose
high, if the fog retreated, we'd hurl shadows.
so I drive with open windows and my meaty
ears hurt. I can't hear ya. I see a carpenter hammering
nails. I see a cat shifting. I see Vladimir
walking up the stairs and I call out, Vladimir!
he turns around, doesn't recognize me. we walk in sync
with the rotation of the world. usually, I'm faster.
I rely on poor technique and poor tactics and
still leave marks behind. once I find someone
as fast as me I'll name him. high above me
crawls a plane. I can't see or hear it, but it's abundantly
clear. from above, the rainbow is lead. it floats in all
those fickle intersections, weightless, yet sinking. tradition
says: walk underneath it! tradition says you're married
your girl is dark, and the Devil is beating his wife. rain has been
brought down, flowers are bloody, animals slack-jawed.
a fly enters through the window. it's quiet. music resists space,
and space follows its notes. bound, it drips through my pores.
every time I drive I remember my own speed. no one
ever ran that way. one time I reached a neighboring
village before a car. it was pouring buckets. the roads were

muddy. I tripped a few times, I was dirt-brown, yet happy.
I never ran again, I wanted to be remembered that way.
I thought of people. it's fiction that my poems contain
no people. there's Vladimir. I called out his Name
and he climbed, to the northern sky. it's noon. our shadows
are behind us, or in front of us. the speed decreases. all
animals have vanished. death is a tradition; it should be bound,
left to rot. we should be more like magnets. love is
rigor. a strict process. I brewed for an entire year.
all year long I brewed tea.

# WAITING FOR THE SONG

You lie down and wait for the song. still.
like a sly glue-coated
branch waiting for a bird.
often a robin, or a finch.
you lurk festive in your silence, quiet
like a robin or a finch
that never arrived.
under the skin of the sheet damp from sweat and breath,
hot from the body, as if you're waiting on a low cloud.
you scratch. twiddle your thumbs, blink, at times
correctly, at times not, but stay still.
outside the winter bites. blood freezes,
skin tightens the back, the wind belts and branches
of oaks scrape the rapids in the fog of windows.
that's all you hear and see. you know between
you and the world stands the glass, that nothing
can land on you. still you lie and wait for the song.
you wait for it.

# ABOUT THE AUTHOR

Marko Pogačar was born in 1984. in Split, Yugoslavia. He is the author of five poetry collections, five books of essays, a short story collection, and a travelogue. He edited the *Young Croatian Lyric* anthology (2014) and is an editor of the literary magazine *Quorum*, and *Proletter*, an online magazine for cultural and social issues. He received, among others, Civitella Ranieri, Literarische Colloquium Berlin, Récollets-Paris, Passa Porta, Milo Dor, Brandenburger Tor, Internationales Haus der Autoren Graz, Literaturhaus NÖ, Krokodil Beograd and Poeteka Tirana scholarships and writer's residences, and is currently a DAAD fellow in Berlin. He received Croatian and international awards for poetry, prose, and essays. His work has been translated into more than thirty languages.

### ORIGINAL EDITIONS:

*Pijavice nad Santa Cruzom*, poetry (AGM, Zagreb 2006)
*Poslanice običnim ljudima*, poetry (Algoritam, Zagreb 2007)
*Predmeti*, poetry (Algoritam, Zagreb 2009)
*Atlas glasova*, essays (V.B.Z, Zagreb 2011)
*Jer mi smo mnogi*, essays (Algoritam, Zagreb, 2011)
*Bog neće pomoći*, short stories (Algoritam, Zagreb, 2012)
*Crna pokrajina*, poetry (Algoritam, Zagreb, 2013)
*Jugoton gori!*, essays (Sandorf, Zagreb, 2013)
*Hrvatska mlada lirika 2014*, anthology (HDP, Zagreb 2014)
*Slijepa karta*, travelogue (Fraktura, Zaprešić 2016)
*Zemlja Zemlja*, poetry (Fraktura, Zaprešić 2017)
*Pobuna čuvara / Čitati noću*, essays (KCNS, Novi Sad 2018)

*Dead Letter Office* contains poems selected from the following collections: *Zemlja Zemlja* (2017), *Crna pokrajina* (2013), *Predmeti* (2009) and *Poslanice običnim ljudima* (2007).

# ABOUT THE TRANSLATOR

Andrea Jurjević grew up in Rijeka, Croatia, in the former Yugoslavia, before immigrating to the United States. Her debut poetry collection, *Small Crimes*, won the 2015 Philip Levine Poetry Prize, and her book-length translations from Croatian include *Mamasafari* (Diálogos Press, 2018).

Her work has appeared, or is forthcoming, in *The Believer*, *TriQuarterly*, *The Missouri Review*, *Gulf Coast* and *The Southeast Review*, among many others. She was the recipient of a Robinson Jeffers Tor Prize, a Tennessee Williams Scholarship from the Sewanee Writers' Conference, a Hambidge Fellowship, and the 2018 Georgia Author of the Year award.

Jurjević lives in Atlanta, Georgia, and teaches at Georgia State University.

# ABOUT THE WORD WORKS

Since its founding in 1974, The Word Works has steadily published volumes of contemporary poetry and presented public programs. Its imprints include The Washington Prize, The Tenth Gate Prize, The Hilary Tham Capital Collection, and International Editions.

Monthly, The Word Works offers free literary programs in the Café Muse series at The Writer's Center in Bethesda, MD, and each summer it holds free poetry programs in Washington, DC's Rock Creek Nature Center. Word Works programs have included "In the Shadow of the Capitol," a symposium and archival project on the African American intellectual community in segregated Washington, DC; the Gunston Arts Center Poetry Series; the Poet Editor panel discussions at The Writer's Center; Master Class work-shops; and a writing retreat in Tuscany, Italy.

As a 501(c)3 organization, The Word Works has received awards from the National Endowment for the Arts, the National Endowment for the Humanities, the D.C. Commission on the Arts & Humanities, the Witter Bynner Foundation, Poets & Writers, The Writer's Center, Bell Atlantic, the David G. Taft Foundation, and others, including many generous private patrons.

It is a member of the Community of Literary Magazines and Presses and its books are distributed by Small Press Distribution.

wordworksbooks.org

# OTHER WORD WORKS BOOKS

Annik Adey-Babinski, *Okay Cool No Smoking Love Pony*
Karren L. Alenier, *Wandering on the Outside*
Karren L. Alenier, ed., *Whose Woods These Are*
Karren L. Alenier & Miles David Moore, eds.,
       *Winners: A Retrospective of the Washington Prize*
Christopher Bursk, ed., *Cool Fire*
Willa Carroll, *Nerve Chorus*
Grace Cavalieri, *Creature Comforts*
Abby Chew, *A Bear Approaches from the Sky*
Nadia Colburn, *The High Shelf*
Henry Crawford, *Binary Planet*
Barbara Goldberg, *Berta Broadfoot and Pepin the Short*
Akua Lezli Hope, *Them Gone*
Frannie Lindsay, *If Mercy*
Elaine Maggarrell, *The Madness of Chefs*
Marilyn McCabe, *Glass Factory*
Kevin McLellan, *Ornitheology*
JoAnne McFarland, *Identifying the Body*
Leslie McGrath, *Feminists Are Passing from Our Lives*
Ann Pelletier, *Letter That Never*
Ayaz Pirani, *Happy You Are Here*
W.T. Pfefferle, *My Coolest Shirt*
Jacklyn Potter, Dwaine Rieves, Gary Stein, eds.,
       *Cabin Fever: Poets at Joaquin Miller's Cabin*
Robert Sargent, *Aspects of a Southern Story*
       *& A Woman from Memphis*
Julia Story, *Spinster for Hire*
Miles Waggener, *Superstition Freeway*
Fritz Ward, *Tsunami Diorama*
Camille-Yvette Welsh, *The Four Ugliest Children in Christendom*
Amber West, *Hen & God*
Maceo Whitaker, *Narco Farm*
Nancy White, ed., *Word for Word*

Nathalie Anderson, *Following Fred Astaire*, 1998
Michael Atkinson, *One Hundred Children Waiting for a
    Train*, 2001
Molly Bashaw, *The Whole Field Still Moving Inside It*, 2013
Carrie Bennett, *biography of water*, 2004
Peter Blair, *Last Heat*, 1999
John Bradley, *Love-in-Idleness: The Poetry of Roberto
    Zingarello*, 1995, 2ND edition 2014
Christopher Bursk, *The Way Water Rubs Stone*, 1988
Richard Carr, *Ace*, 2008
Jamison Crabtree, *Rel[AM]ent*, 2014
Jessica Cuello, *Hunt*, 2016
Barbara Duffey, *Simple Machines*, 2015
B. K. Fischer, *St. Rage's Vault*, 2012
Linda Lee Harper, *Toward Desire*, 1995
Ann Rae Jonas, *A Diamond Is Hard But Not Tough*, 1997
Annie Kim, *Eros, Unbroken*, 2019
Susan Lewis, *Zoom*, 2017
Frannie Lindsay, *Mayweed*, 2009
Richard Lyons, *Fleur Carnivore*, 2005
Elaine Magarrell, *Blameless Lives*, 1991
Fred Marchant, *Tipping Point*, 1993, 2ND edition 2013
Nils Michals, *Gembox*, 2018
Ron Mohring, *Survivable World*, 2003
Barbara Moore, *Farewell to the Body*, 1990
Brad Richard, *Motion Studies*, 2010
Jay Rogoff, *The Cutoff*, 1994
Prartho Sereno, *Call from Paris*, 2007, 2ND edition 2013
Enid Shomer, *Stalking the Florida Panther*, 1987
John Surowiecki, *The Hat City After Men Stopped Wearing
    Hats*, 2006
Miles Waggener, *Phoenix Suites*, 2002
Charlotte Warren, *Gandhi's Lap*, 2000
Mike White, *How to Make a Bird with Two Hands*, 2011
Nancy White, *Sun, Moon, Salt*, 1992, 2ND edition 2010
George Young, *Spinoza's Mouse*, 1996

Nathalie Anderson, *Stain*
Mel Belin, *Flesh That Was Chrysalis*
Carrie Bennett, *The Land Is a Painted Thing*
Doris Brody, *Judging the Distance*
Sarah Browning, *Whiskey in the Garden of Eden*
Grace Cavalieri, *Pinecrest Rest Haven*
Cheryl Clarke, *By My Precise Haircut*
Christopher Conlon, *Gilbert and Garbo in Love*
           & *Mary Falls: Requiem for Mrs. Surratt*
Donna Denizé, *Broken Like Job*
W. Perry Epes, *Nothing Happened*
David Eye, *Seed*
Bernadette Geyer, *The Scabbard of Her Throat*
Elizabeth Gross, *this body / that lightning show*
Barbara G. S. Hagerty, *Twinzilla*
Lisa Hase-Jackson, *Flint & Fire*
James Hopkins, *Eight Pale Women*
Donald Illich, *Chance Bodies*
Brandon Johnson, *Love's Skin*
Thomas March, *Aftermath*
Marilyn McCabe, *Perpetual Motion*
Judith McCombs, *The Habit of Fire*
James McEwen, *Snake Country*
Miles David Moore, *The Bears of Paris* & *Rollercoaster*
Kathi Morrison-Taylor, *By the Nest*
Tera Vale Ragan, *Reading the Ground*
Michael Shaffner, *The Good Opinion of Squirrels*
Maria Terrone, *The Bodies We Were Loaned*
Hilary Tham, *Bad Names for Women* & *Counting*
Barbara Ungar, *Charlotte Brontë, You Ruined My Life*
           & *Immortal Medusa*
Jonathan Vaile, *Blue Cowboy*
Rosemary Winslow, *Green Bodies*
Kathleen Winter, *Transformer*
Michele Wolf, *Immersion*
Joe Zealberg, *Covalence*

## INTERNATIONAL EDITIONS

Kajal Ahmad (Alana Marie Levinson-LaBrosse, Mewan
  Nahro Said Sofi, and Darya Abdul-Karim Ali Najin,
  trans., with Barbara Goldberg), *Handful of Salt*
Liliana Ancalao (Seth Michelson, trans.), *Women of the Big Sky*
Keyne Cheshire (trans.), *Murder at Jagged Rock:*
  *A Tragedy by Sophocles*
Jeannette L. Clariond (Curtis Bauer, trans.), *Image of Absence*
Jean Cocteau (Mary-Sherman Willis, trans.), *Grace Notes*
Yoko Danno & James C. Hopkins, *The Blue Door*
Moshe Dor (Barbara Goldberg, trans.), *Scorched by the Sun*
Moshe Dor, Barbara Goldberg, Giora Leshem, eds.,
  *The Stones Remember: Native Israeli Poets*
Laura Cesarco Eglin (Jesse Lee Kercheval and Catherine
  Jagoe, rans.), *Reborn in Ink*
Vladimir Levchev (Henry Taylor, trans.), *Black Book of the
  Endangered Species*
Marko Pogačar (Andrea Jurjević, trans.), *Dead Letter Office*
Lee Sang (Myong-Hee Kim, trans.) *Crow's Eye View: The
  Infamy of Lee Sang, Korean Poet*

## THE TENTH GATE PRIZE

Jennifer Barber, *Works on Paper*, 2015
Lisa Lewis, *Taxonomy of the Missing*, 2017
Brad Richard, *Parasite Kingdom*, 2018
Roger Sedarat, *Haji As Puppet*, 2016
Lisa Sewell, *Impossible Object*, 2014